PORTUGUESE COOKBOOK

1

SUSAN SAM

TABLE OF CONTENTS

Portuguese Buns

Portuguese Rice Pudding

Saucy Portuguese Fillet (Perfect For Rolls And Burgers)

Portuguese Custard Tarts

Portuguese Custard Tarts (Natas) With Blood Orange Caramel

Portuguese Chicken Curry

Farturas (Portuguese-Style Donuts)

Portuguese Cod

Portuguese Hake

Portuguese Chicken Stew

Portuguese Peri Peri Chicken

Beef A Casa (Portuguese Steak)

Portuguese Orange-Cinnamon Cake

Cod Fish With Fries

Portuguese Stew

Homemade Portuguese Rolls

Portuguese Rice

Portuguese Linguica And Green Beans

INTRODUCTION

The Portuguese cuisine also provides strong People from france and Mediterranean affects. Especially in the wide range of spices or herbs are used in many traditional candy and some hot and spicy dishes. Olive essential oil is one of the bases of Portuguese cuisine, which is utilized both for cooking and flavouring meals.

Portuguese often consume grain, taters, and breads using their foods and there are many types of traditional fresh bread like broa which might offer local and national variants within the countries under Lusophone or Galician influence.

1. Saffron Portuguese Serradura

Ingredients

10-12 Marie biscuits
1 cup fresh cream
1/2 cup condensed milk
1 pinch saffron
2 tsp milk

For garnishing :
As required pistachios powder
As needed splitted cashew nuts
As needed saffron strands

Directions

To start with saturate the saffron follicle in the for 10 minutes.
Work the biscuits to make crumbs.
Mix the cream for sometime with the aid of a hand blender.
After that add condensed dairy and saffron dairy in it and again blend it well for 2-3 minutes.
Then have a glass and set biscuit breadcrumbs at the end of the cup and make a layer of it.
Then pour some saffron mixed cream over the top of it.
Nonetheless some biscuit breadcrumbs.
Like that make layer up-to the very best of the glass.
After that garnish which includes pista powder, splitted cashew nuts and saffron strands over the top of it.
This treat is ready and then maintain it in the refrigerator for 2-3 hours.
After that enjoy endlessly this Portuguese style treat.

2. Portuguese Sausage And Rice

Ingredients

2 Cups Rice Long Grain
1/4 Cup Celery chopped
5 - 6 Chicken Franks (chopped)
1 Cup Cilantro Coriander Leaves
1/2 Cup Tomato Chopped
1 Onion chopped
2 Tablespoons Paprika
3 - 4 Cups Water

Directions

Inside a huge container, temperature a little essential oil and toss in the onion, tomato, cilantro and oatmeal. Saute them quickly.

At this point add sodium to taste and the paprika. Blend well.

Add Drinking drinking water (Measure out the water with respect to the food preparation teaching of the grain).

Add the chicken franks and accept the water up to boil. After the drinking water has hard hard boiled, add the wheat. Accept water returning to boil. Once it has hard boiled, lower the fire to a simmer and close the entire container.

Permit the grain prepare for about a quarter-hour. Provide with ketchup.

3. Portuguese Jag With Shrimp, Clams And Linguica

Ingredients

1 cup long grain white rice
1/2 cup frozen or canned lima beans
1 tbsp chopped yellow onions
1 tblsp of chopped garlic
1 tsp seasalt
1 tsp black pepper
1/2 of slices Linguica
one tblsp of olive oil or Avocado oil
6 little neck Clams
6 Jumbo Shrimp
cups of Kale for decorating
2 cups water
4 tbsp butter

Directions

Inside a huge saute skillet add olive until it heats up at add onions saute for one minute or 2 add drinking water, rice and lima put on heat range till it comes to a steam put cover on and change to low and prepare for 30 minutes. Within a medium saute skillet add butter and garlic clove saute until aromatic don't burn off, add clam juice once considering a simmer add clams and Shrimp and linguica, you can saute Linguica in a separate frying pan to obtain a sear to them.

Once clams place open up and shrimp is red and prepared through put apart.

Get a plate place Grain and beans in it then top with clams. Linguica and shrimp decorate with Kale and enjoy.

4. Arroz Doce (Portuguese Sweet Rice)

Ingredients

3 cups milk
1 cup water
1/2 cup sugar
1 cup arborio rice (the rice you use for risotto)
two slices lemon zest (about the size of your thumb)
2 egg yolks
Cinnamon for dusting

Directions

In a very very pot, bring dairy, water and " lemon " zest in purchase to boil.

Add your rice and prepare on moderate to medium low, mixing often.

When the rice is certainly almost fully prepared and still merely a little al dente, add your sugar. Cook for 3 or more more min.

Remove from heat and stir in your egg yolks, blending quickly/vigorously for couple of seconds until well combined.

Pour in to dish/platter and add cinnamon.

Enjoy in fact any way, scorching, room temp or cold. (I select room temp yet will eat this any way)

5.   My Portuguese Style Rice

Ingredients

2 cups basmati rice
2 1/4 cups cold water
1 red onion diced
1/2 juice of a lemon
1 red chilli diced
1 chicken stock cube
2 tbsp tomato puree
1 tsp turmeric powder
1 tsp cumin
2 tsp smoked paprika
1 tsp oregano
2 tsp garlic powder
1 tsp parsley
1 tsp red chilli flakes
to taste Salt and pepper

Directions

The simple cut vegies.
Put grain, share cube, tomato blend, water, spices and veg into a pot blend well, provide for a steam then cover with a tight installing cover and prepare for 10 mins.
Once ready allow to steam for 5 minutes, then mix well
Serve and enjoy!

6. Portuguese Custard Tarts

Ingredients

1 Puff Pastry
2 Tablespoons Soft Butter
1/3 Cup Flour
1 1/2 Cup Milk
1 1/3 Cup Sugar
1/3 Cup Water
4 Large Egg yolks
1 Teaspoon Vanilla Essence
1 Cinnamon Stick
2/3 Orange Peels

Directions

Pre-specified the your oven to 220° C and lightly oil a 12-cup muffin pot.

In a saucepan, provide a steam the glucose, drinking water, vanilla eximportance, lemon peels, and cinnamon stick. Prepare until boils. Withstand the to mix. Individually, whisk the dairy and flour collectively very completely. Prepare over medium temperature, whisking constantly, for about 5 minutes or until well combined and the milk is thickened. Take off the heat and let cool for ten minutes.

Once cooled down off, whisk in the egg yolks. There after add the glucose syrup (first removing the cinnamon stay and lemon peels), and combine until everything is well-combined. Strain into a measuring container.

Meanwhile, turns away the puff pastry linen and clean within the melted butter. Tightly move the sheet into a log, from the short aspect. Following, cut the sign in 12 evenly size parts.

Place one piece in each one of the 12 wells of the muffin container. Sinking your thumb in cold drinking drinking water first, press your thumb into the middle of the dough piece and press outwards to create a glass with the pastry. The pastry glass must have the top advantage just above the very best of the well of the muffin container. Fill up each pastry glass 3/4 of the greatest way to the most effective with the custard mixture.

Put the tray in the oven and cook until the custard commences to caramelize and sore and the pastry will go golden dark dark brown (roughly 15-20 minutes).

Serve warm, with powdered sugar and ground cinnamon (both optional, but delicious)! Enjoy!

7. Portuguese Chicken

Ingredients

Chicken pieces with skin, I usually just use about four
breasts and two drumsticks
1 tsp Salt (to taste)
1 tsp ginger and garlic paste
Half bottle Portuguese peri peri sauce
1 tsp chillie flakes
1 tsp coarse black pepper
500 ml fresh cream or less depending on chicken quantity

Directions

Water vapor chicken pieces by 50 % cup boiling water, water vapor with ginger and garlic paste and 1 teaspoon sodium.

Once chicken is steamed, remove from the stove.

In a bowl mix in the fresh cream with Portuguese sauce, add in chillie flakes and black peper.

Layer chicken with 50 pct the spices or herbs or herbs.

Upon a hot barbeque grill drizzle olive oil, place the chicken items, keep basting with sauce and change over until well grilled.

Remove chicken, for the relax of the spices or herbs use it the grill and then poir it over the barbequed poultry, this provides excellent taste.

Provide with green greens, Portuguese rolls and french fries.

8. Biscoitos (Portuguese Cookies)

Ingredients

1 cup butter, softened
1.5 cups sugar
5 eggs
5 cups flour
4 tsp Baking Powder

Directions

Combine the Butter, Bloodstream sugar and ovum in a substantial dish. Defeat everything collectively after medium-high acceleration till everything is rich and rich and rich and creamy. About 40 sec- 1 min.

Place the dry substances into the moist and beat until everything is combined.

Cover with plastic-type material wrap and refrigerate for about two hr. (Firming in the breads in the refrigerator demands less mess when rolling them to could be baked)

When ready to bake: take regarding half a teaspoon of money, move between hands and design into a lengthy pipe, attach both ends to produce an corporation. (or any kind of design you like)

Cook in preheated 350ºF oven related to 18-20 min till softly browned.

Established on cooling stand to cool totally.

So great fallen in espresso. Dough may be refrigerated up to three times.

9. Caldo Verde Com Chourico (Portuguese Collard Green Garden Soup)

Ingredients

2 tbs extra virgin olive oil
1 chourico,linguica or Spanish chorizo sliced in 0.25 inch rounds
1 large onion, diced
to taste Salt and white pepper
3 garlic cloves, minced
6 large potatoes, peeled and chopped
four cups chicken stock AND three cups of water
one pound (medium bunch) collard greens or kale, sliced thin

Directions

Inside a sizable container, add your olive petrol and dark brown the chourico on medium heat. Enable the fat from the sausage to really come away as this helps flavour the soups. Once done, remove chourico with placed spoon make apart.

Add the onions and cook until clear, then add your garlic. Mix to combine.

Add your raw taters to the container, mix then add your water and poultry broth. Provide everything to a steam, then reduce temperature and let simmer until the taters are shell sensitive.

Employing a wand blender, blend the soup to a smooth persistence. You want it mainly smooth but a few LITTLE spud pieces are fine.

Season with sodium and pepper to your flavor. Add your collard produce (or kale) along with your choirico back again to the pot and bring back again again up to simply boil, then reduce heat and let simmer for three-five min. Provide with bread if desired.

10. Portuguese Rolls

Ingredients

4 cups sifted plain flour
2 tsp salt
4 tsp sugar
1 pkt dry yeast(10g)
3 Tbs olive or veg oil
2 cups lukewarm water

Dusting:
Flour

Directions

Within a bowl, sort the dry elements. Make a well and add the essential oil then warm drinking water. Mix together with your hands to create a simple dough. Whether is really too sticky put in place a little more flour. Knead the cash for 10mins.

Cover the bowl with plastic and keep it in a warm area to rise for one hour. Knead for three mins then divide the dough into 12/13 oval balls. Make a slit in the heart of every with a knife then dirt the dough with flour. Cover an additional 30/40mins till this proofs.

Preheat the oven at 200°c and bake the rolls for 15mins till golden brown. Allow it to cool then place in place a plastic handbag later on or provide warm.

11. Portuguese Donuts

Ingredients

1/4 cup butter
1 tablespoon sugar
1 cup water
1 cup all purpose wheat flour
1 pinch salt
Cardamon (for taste)
4 eggs
Oil for frying
Sugar for coating/ Icing sugar

Directions

Add butter, water, sugar and cardamon in a pot and bring to vapor. Turn of the heat and blend in the flour. Stir in the flour until it forms a ball. Let it cool.
Add your ovum one-by-one while stiring to produce a batter.
Heat your oil in a pan. Drop your donuts in the oil you might use a tsp. Fry until gently brown.
Move them in the sugars while warm and serve.

12. Portuguese Chicken

Ingredients

3 pound whole chicken
Peri Peri sauce (Can choose as your deal)

Directions

Cut along one part of backbone and split open chicken. Flatten chicken lower limbs and upper thighs merely by pushing down after them make metal skewers crosswise in a one breast to the other in the very best and one thigh to the other in the underside.

Oil barbeque grill with nonstick cooking spray and after that high temperature barbeque grill to 550 levels.

Change off 1 burner make the other 2 writers on medium warmth. Prepare chicken after roundabout heat (burner that has been converted off) to get 20 minutes with breast side entirely down.

Carry on and cook after indirect heat to get 20 minutes with breast aspect up.

Brush poultry with Peri spices and prepare to get 5 more instances on each part (10 minutes total) on indirect warmth. After that brush after more sauce and prepare for five more minutes after each side (10 minutes total) after immediate heat (burners that are on). Internal temperature of meats should become 165 degrees F when done.

Provide with more sauce to get dipping as well as your much-loved side meals.

Appreciate!

13. Portuguese Buns

Ingredients

4 cups flour
2 Tblsp instant yeast
1/3 cup sugar
1 tsp salt
1 cup warm milk
0.5 cup warm fresh cream (can use milk instead)
5 Tblsp softened butter
1 egg
Flour for dusting

Directions

Combine 3 cups of flour, yeast, sugar, salt, warm dairy products, cream, butter, and egg in the bowl of a stand mixer. (Make sure milk is usually warm as this is what triggers the yeast)

Using the money attach turn the mixing machine onto the lowest speed until flour is built-in, scraping over the edges of the dish as necessary.

Boost speed to moderate and defeat designed for 2 minutes. (can be kneaded by simply hand as well)

Add 1/2 glass flour and mix and then add another 1/2 glass flour and replicate, mixing at moderate speed for an additional 2 minutes till a ball of money is created.

The dough ought to be slightly sticky and soft and pulling definately not the good thing about the dish. Transfer the money to a gently greased bowl and cover with cling film. Let rise intended for 30 minutes in room temperature.

Deflate the dough by simply striking down gently. Touch off aspects of the money and form sixteen buns. (can become made smaller intended for slider buns, etc)

Transfer the comes to a lightly greased baking dish. (For pot buns, dust tray with flour first. Place buns, then sprinkle flour on best again) Cover with cling film once again and let rise for an extra 30 minutes in room temperature.

Pre-specified the oven to at least one hundred and 80 degrees. Bake the rolls for 12 to 15 memories or until fantastic brown and ready through.

For regular rolls or buns: Remove rolls and brush hot will go along with the melted butter. Provide immediately!

14. Portuguese Rice Pudding

Ingredients

1 L 3% (Homogenized) milk
1 L Water
1/4 lb Butter (unsalted preferably)
2 tsp Salt
Sliced up zest of small lemon (count bits of zest to ensure that all are removed later)
1.25 cup Arborio or Carolina Rice, soaked in water
1 cup + 3 TBS white sugar
6 Egg Yolks
Cinnamon (for garnish)

Directions

Cover with water and soak the wheat in a small dish (not the same water since below) and established apart. Combine dairy, drinking water, butter, salt and " lemon " in a large pot. Be sure to count factors of zest to make certain that all are removed later.

Offer contents of pot in order to a steam using medium temperature.

When milk comes drain the grain from the first stage and add this to milk.

TAKE NOTICE VERY CAREFULY -- IMPORTANT STEP!!! Combine a couple of times to blend then leave upon LOWEST heat WITH NO STIRRING until wheat grains come toward the top of liquid, it will eventually appearance almost solid. This takes at least one hour and perhaps longer in line with the sort of rice utilized. Verify that the rice is gentle. If not, keep a lttle little bit longer. Remove parts of lemon zeal.

Add Sugar and mix pot pertaining to 2 to several minutes to melt.

Gently beat and add 6 egg yolks.

On the second start stirring continuously until mixture thickens and looks wealthy and creamy, regarding 5 mins.

Put into a large heatproof dish or several smaller foods, add cinnamon and let cool.

15. Saucy Portuguese Fillet (Perfect For Rolls And Burgers)

Ingredients

one kg fillet- butterfly and cut into small flat pieces

Marinade Chicken fillet in:
1 tsp fine Salt
Crushed black pepper
1/2 tsp turmeric powder
1 tsp garlic paste
1 tsp cajun spice
2 tsp red chilli powder
1 tsp Portuguese /chicken spice of choice
3 tbsp Portuguese sauce
1 tsp crushed chillies
1 tsp lemon pepper
1 tblsp honey/golden syrup

Directions

Marinate for at least an hour and leave in refrigerator. Within a cooking pan, pour in some oil to shallow fry. Once hot, range from the poultry and smolder until done, flicking to brown both edges.
Put in place a container and add bit of water and a tblsp of inch lemon " juice cover with container lid and leave to vapor for 5-10mins. If you think there is certainly water remaining, allow it to run dry. Place poultry pieces in oven tray. (i still left it inside a pot that works extremely well in oven as well)

To get the sauce:
High temperature blob of butter, add in a sprinkle of Sodium and also Pepper.
3 tblsp Portuguese sauce
five tblsp fresh cream
2tbsp pasta sauce
Red colouring

I actually also added any remaining marinate through the chicken to the sauce Optionally available: include a tblsp of chilli spices if u appreciate it sizzling.

Provide it a steam and remove from high temperature.

Pour more than fillet pieces.

Temperatures in oven and grill if popular.

16. Portuguese Custard Tarts

Ingredients

2 sheets puff pastry
1 Tbsp cinnamon
2 eggs
2 Tbsp sugar
2 tsp vanilla
1 C creme fraiche
2 Tbsp orange zest

Directions

Spread puff pastry sheets with a moving pin. Sprinkle with cinnamon and carefully rub it in, spreading it similarly.

Roll-up both pastry sheets tightly, large ending facing you, and cut each into 6 even items.

Stand up each piece on its ending and flatten down with fingers, place hard disks in standard muffin pan. Using convenience, spread each piece into a cup condition using the pan as a mold. Bake for 8-10 minutes at 200 in oven on top stand.

Custard mix: In a very very medium size dish mix with the other eggs, sugar, vanilla, creme fraiche and orange zest.

Get muffin tray away of the oven and by by using a tea spoon test their limitations the pastry into the mold and into its cup condition so it retains the custard. Fill up each covering almost to the top with custard combine. Put custard-filled pastry shells back to the oven on the top rack and cook for 8-10 minutes. Move tarts on to wire rack to cool.

17. Portuguese Custard Tarts (Natas) With Blood Orange Caramel

Ingredients

1 sheet ready roll puff pastry
2 teaspoons Cinnamon
7 tablespoons caster sugar
1 orange
120 g crime fresh
1 egg
Vanilla essence

Directions

Heart stroke the cinnamon and a little little bit of sugars on to the sheet of pastry. Once dusted switch over and move lengthways. Cut the roll in to 6-7 pieces. Push the dough in to all the muffin tin adjusts, producing a small well in the middle of each tart. Once ready bake in a preheated oven for 8-10 a few minutes until the pastry is virtually prepared

As the tarts are in the oven prepare the custard. Combining jointly the egg, cream fresh, lemon zeal, vanilla fact and a tea spoon of sugar.

Consider away the tarts in the oven. Squash the middle with the again from the tea spoon to change the wells. Put the custard to the well and get back to the oven for 8-10 minutes.

Because the tarts are in the oven once more, warm up a no stick skillet and add the six tablespoons of sugars and a press of fifty per cent the orange. To produce a caramel. Top the tarts with the lemon colored caramel and established aside to great.

18. Portuguese Chicken Curry

Ingredients

1 large onion, finely chopped
3 garlic cloves, finely chopped
1 tbsp lard or 2 tbsp oil
2 tbsp olive oil
1 carrot, peeled and sliced
1 Green bell pepper, finely chopped
To taste dried or fresh chillies
to taste Salt
6-8 chicken pieces
100 ml hot chicken stock
50 ml white wine
400 ml coconut milk
5 tsp curry powder
1 tsp coriander powder
6-8 small potatoes, peeled (optional)

Directions

Friendliness the olive gas and oil or lard in a saucepan or wok.

Add the red onion, and smolder until soft and clear, about three to four minutes. Add the garlic clove and help another minute of cooking.

Add the chicken items, skin side down and add 2 teaspoons of Curry powder. Add the dried chilli and season with sodium. Allow to smolder for 3-5 minutes then stir.

Add the carrot and green pepper and invite to smolder for an additional few minutes. Add your wine and prepare for 5 minutes.

Add the chicken stock and prepare for an additional 5 minutes.

Add 3 more tsps of Curry natural powder, coriander powder and the coconut dairy. Cover the skillet with a cover and invite to simmer higher than a low warmth for 35-40 minutes. Add the taters in 25 to fifty percent an hour before turning heat off.

Serve with basmati rice.

19. Farturas (Portuguese-Style Donuts)

Ingredients

2 cups plain flour
2 cups water
2 tbsp butter
3 tbsp sugar
1 large egg, beaten
Zest of 1 lemon
1 tsp baking powder
as needed Cooking oil
1 tsp salt
as needed Sweet cinnamon powder
as needed Caster Sugar

Directions

Offer the boil in a very very medium to large saucepan drinking drinking water, sugar, butter, inch lemon " zeal and sodium.

Remove from the warmth and add the flour, combining continuously. Continue preparing food for 4-5 instances more than a medium warmth. Allow to awesome slightly, enough to take care of together with your hands.

Add the egg and baking natural natural powder to the combo and using your hands mix well.

Heat the deep fat fryer.

Place the mixture appropriate into a water lines bag and carefully pipe straight to the oil till fantastic brown.

Inside a bowl blend some cinnamon and glucose together.

And series a dish which includes kitchen move.

Take aside the farturas to the home dish lined with kitchen roll.

Sprinkle a few cinnamon sugar to the farturas since they come away of the fryer.

Best offered moderately dewrinkled.

20. Portuguese Cod

Ingredients

6 pieces cod, frozen thawed
1 (28 oz) can whole tomatoes Italian
1 (16 oz) can diced tomatoes
1 cup pitted Kalamata olives
4 crushed garlic cloves
4 tablespoons capers
to taste Salt and pepper
2 tablespoons Italian dried herbs

Directions

Unfreeze cod and place in 8x12 cooking food dish. Heat oven to 400F.

In large sauté frying pan add olive important oil and garlic clove and warm more than low warmth.

Place tomato vegetables in pan and hands crush 28oz may of entire tomato vegetables. Add capers and olives (diced). Awesome on medium warmth for 10-20mins until flavors blend and taste is somewhat salty.

Put spices over seafood and bake found out intended for 20 minutes.

Appreciate with ciabatta breads rubbed with garlic clove and necessary intended for oven.

21. Portuguese Hake

Ingredients

1 box hake medallions
Salt and pepper (to taste)
1 Tbsp butter
1 tsp garlic paste
6 Tbsp Portuguese marinade
1/2 cup fresh cream
Dried parsley (garnish)

Directions

Defrost and gently press water out among flat palms.
Period with pinch salt and pepper and fry with a drizzle
of important oil till nearly done. Remove from skillet.
Add butter to pan, saute garlic clove, after that add in the
dressing and high heat range through.
Add in cream and provide to boil.
Add fish into the pan and enable sauce to thicken.
When serving, place extra sauce in a gravy motorboat and
serve along with the fish.
(Do not really add any sodium, lemon or chillies to spices
as it is extremely well seasoned already.)

22. Portuguese Chicken Stew

Ingredients

6 chicken pieces, bone-in, skin on
1 large onion, chopped
150 ml white wine
100 g unsalted butter
3 garlic cloves, chopped
1 chicken stock cube
to taste Salt
1 large carrot, peeled and sliced
2 Bay leaves
1 tbsp tomato puree

Directions

Heat range the butter in a very very saucepan more than a medium/high high temperature. Brownish the poultry well.

Next add the onion, garlic clove, these kind of leaves and share cube.

Cover with lid and permit to simmer to get 5 mins or until the red red onion has softened.

Subsequent add the oatmeal. Cook another five mins.

Add the tomato puree and wine.

Carry on and simmer more than a medium temperature for 20-30 mins or until the chicken and celery are prepared through.

Check spices. Modify if needed. Remove the these types of leaves and provide with rice or hard boiled taters.

23. Portuguese Peri Peri Chicken

Ingredients

3 bird eye red chilies
5 garlic cloves
3 Tbsp oil
4 tbsp vinegar
2 tbsp paprika
1 tbsp dried oregano
1/2 tsp garlic powder
1 tsp mustard powder
1 large red pepper
1 1/2 tsp sugar
Salt black pepper to taste
Orange & red food colour

Sauce:
2 tblsp lemon juice
3 tblsp butter
2 tsp garlic
1 tsp paprika

2 tsp parsley
1/2 cup Peri peri sauce
2 tblsp tomato puree
2 tblsp mayonnaise
1/2 cup Fresh cream

Peri Peri Sauce:
3 birds eye red chilies
1 large red pepper
5 garlic cloves
3 tbsp oil
4 tbsp vinegar
2 tbsp paprika
1 tbsp dried oregano
1/2 tsp garlic powder
2 tsp onion powder
1 tsp mustard powder
1 1/2 tsp sugar
salt to taste
Black pepper
red orange food colour

Directions

Place the Peri Sauce elements within a food blender and mix till smooth. Blend most the constituents and marinate 1 poultry for at least one hour.
Prepare on stove until water dry.
From then on add sauce and grill in the oven.
Mix most sauce ingredients within a sauce skillet.
Give a steam. Add coriander. Put over cooked poultry and grill.

24. Beef A Casa (Portuguese Steak)

Ingredients

meat marinade
four pieces steak/fillet (any cut) beaten/tenderized to 0.5 inch
2 tsp chili flakes
1 tbsp olive oil
2 tbsp red wine
to taste Salt and pepper
3 garlic cloves, crushed
1 small onion, thin sliced

ADD INs
4 eggs
1 tbsp olive oil
French fries, as much because you want (baked or fried)

Directions

In a very very bowl, incorporate your meat with all the current dressing ingredients and let marinade meant for 1-2 hours.
Prepare off (or fry) your French france fries make apart. (Don't make this happen too soon to enable them to not be cold)
Add 1 tbsp essential olive petrol to skillet, hot temperature until smoking and then lay your meat and cook/brown your fillet meats 2min per aspect (pour a few of the dressing towards the top to assist along with the planning food and add flavour). Once done established on dish (don't overlap the fillets in home plate.)
In the same pan, prepare your eggs sunnyside up or more easy. Once performed, set an drive top of every part of steak.
Offer hot with french fries and a cold beer! It had been easy!

25. Portuguese Orange-Cinnamon Cake

Ingredients

Dough:
1/2 cup + 5 tbsp of melted and cooled butter
1/8 cup milk
1/2 cup + 4 tbsp of Orange Juice with pulp
1/8 cup Brandy or Rum (for cooking or regular)
1/2 tsp salt
1 yeast packet
4 Cups flour

Filling:
0.5 cup and five tbsp of melted butter
1 cup brown sugar
1 tbsp ground cinnamon
1 tsp fennel seeds chopped
2 tbsp Orange juice

Directions

Intended for the Dough: Combine the dry substances in the dish of the electric mixer fitted with the dough capture attachment. In a separate bowl, defeat together the drinking water ingredients until combined. Pour water to the dry blend and turn into into the combining machine on medium swiftness. Every cohesive bread is created, carry on and knead in the mixer designed for about five a few minutes. Cover with plastic-type material and ask to increase in warm place until double in proportions, about an hour. 5.
Intended for the Filling up: Mix all the substances together in a medium dish.

To construct: Butter an 8-inch ring mold or cake frying pan make in the sheet tray. Clean the dough on to a gently floured surface and dab into a rectangular shape. Cut the bread into 12 pieces, then roll every sq . into a ball. Utilize a moving pin to move each bread ball into a slim circle regarding eight inches in size. This does not need to get specific.

Place one group of money in the bottom level of the skillet or ring mildew. Spread about 1 ½ tablespoons of filling along with the dough. Give it a try again layering and filling with all the current staying, finishing with all the current filling up on best.

Cover the skillet or ring mould with plastic and allow to enhance in a warm place for about 45 minutes. Preheat the oven to 375°F.

Cook the folar for forty five minutes. Enable the wedding cake to cool for some minutes, after that turn the skillet inverted or remove to music group mol as the gooey filling is unquestionably still hot. When you have any type of trouble with this, how to use counter spatula to produce the edges in the wedding cake from the skillet. Cut in to pieces and supply warm or ensuite temp.

26. Cod Fish With Fries

Ingredients

1 Midsize Cod fillet
1 Onion
2 Big potatoes
1 Garlic head
Parsley
Olive Oil

Directions

Keep the cod 48 hours under water just before starting to prepare years old remove the extra of salt.

Steam the cod fillet untill it is incredibly gentle and completely white. Get rid of the pores and skin and mince. This with a covering. (be careful to take out all the spines)

Cut the taters and the red onion in to thin pieces.

Deep fry the taters and save a few of the important extra virgin olive oil.

In a separate pan smolder the onion about five minutes, after that add the carrots and the cod.

Keep frying and smashing the blend untill it offers got the same yellow color, ought to be around 15 minutes.

Serve and appreciate!

27. Portuguese Stew

Ingredients

1 lb Italian sausage
1 onion, chopped
1 bunch kale, chopped
5 cloves garlic, minced
2 tbsp olive oil
2 red potatoes, diced
1 can garbanzo beans, undrained
1 can black beans, partially drained
1 can diced tomatoes, undrained
4 cups chicken or beef broth
1 lemon, juiced
1 PKG chili seasoning
Parmesan cheese, garnish
Croutons, garnish

Directions

Inside a sizable container, add olive essential oil and sausage. Prepare on medium high high temperature. When sausage is nearly cooked, add red onion, garlic and kale. Cook about five min until kale starts to wilt down. Add taters, canned espresso coffee beans and tomatoes, broth, chili seasoning and lemon juice. Convert heat high. Once boiling, turn temperature to low and cover. Simmer around one hour till potatoes are mild.
Garnish with Parmesan and croutons!
Be aware: if you possess a cheese rind laying around, toss it inside your soups. I acquired an asiago rind.

28. Homemade Portuguese Rolls

Ingredients

8 cups flour
1 packet yeast
3 table spoon sugar
1 teaspoon salts
1 teaspoon butter
1 litre warm water

Directions

Add all ingredients in bowl.
Knead this until its clean.
Put it upon the sun to get an hour to raise.
Then you cut it upon a round styles, you can cut it little upon top to decorate it.
You place on oven 180c for 15 -20 minutes.
Then the ready to offer.

29. Portuguese Rice

Ingredients

1 lb Linguica, or more if you want, diced to small pieces
1 Medium Onion, diced
2 cloves Garlic, diced
to taste Ground black pepper
1 tsp Paprika
2-3 Bay Leaves
1 can No Salt Added Diced Tomatoes, 14.5oz
1 tbsp Fresh or Dried Parsley
2 1/4 Cups Water
1 1/2 Cups Jasmine Rice

Directions

Consider those diced Linguica and cook inside a frying frying pan over medium hot temperature. Cook until relatively browned. Remove in the pan to allow cool. Layer beneath of the moderate pot with important olive petrol. Making use of a medium hot temperature, high temperature the oil for around 2 minutes.

Add the onions, garlic clove, black pepper, paprika, and these kind of leaves. Saute the red onion mix until the onions are relatively soft and clear.

Add the tomato vegetables towards the red onion mix and prepare together for regarding 5 mins. After that add the parsley to the entire pot, prepare meant for another minute or two.

And then add the water to drink to the container and offer a boil. Once everything is cooking, add the grain. Remove the these types of leaves.

Stir the grain to combine everything together, after that cover the complete pot, and minimize the warmth to low. Prepare for 15 minutes.

Add the linguica to the container, stir to incorporate together, cover once again, and prepare one more 5 minutes. Work the crispy grain on the bottom, then cook 10 to 15 a few minutes instead.

When performed, stir once and let sit straight down for approximately five minutes. That specifically like you may wait so extremely long. If not really and also you do not brain hot grain, after that dig in!

Provide and indulge in!

30. Portuguese Linguica And Green Beans

Ingredients

one Smoke Portuguese Linguica sausage,chopped in large 1 inch pieces

three large potatoes, skin removed and diced medium-large pieces

1 tbsp tomato paste

1 onion, chopped

two clove garlic, sliced super thin (or minced)

1 can diced tomatoes (796 ml)

one tsp Portuguese Pimenta pepper (or half tsp cayenne and half tsp paprika) *or more if you like it a lil spicier*

salt and pepper

1 tsp olive oil, extra virgin

three cup Fresh green beans (ends removed and cut in half)

water (enough to just cover everything)

Directions

In a pot, heat olive essential oil and Sautee onion and garlic until translucent.

Put your chorico, Portuguese pepper (or cayenne and paprika mix) and tomato substance. Cook 2 min.

Add your potatoes and diced tomatoes (including liquid). Cook 5 min.

Add just enough water to cover everything. Bring to boil and cook over medium heat for about fifteen-twenty min until the potatoes are about 0.75 cooked. Season with salt and pepper.

Put your green coffee beans, let everything come to boil and cook until taters are done and green beans are cooked but still a tad sharp. (you can prepare until green coffee beans don't have quality, but it's always nice when fresh veggies retain their crunch) Serve with Portuguese buns for dipping or any crusty bread (I could literally drink this soup/stew broth!)

NOTE/Optional: when you add the green beans you could also Crack an ovum on top. The spicy liquid will cook the egg through and it's yummy!

Printed in Great Britain
by Amazon

40448648R00040